RIGA
VACATION GUIDE
2023

The Essential and Ultimate Guide to Riga's Hotels, Cuisines, Shopping Tips, Insider's Tips, Top Attractions, History, and Culture

ALFRED FLORES

Copyright © 2023, Alfred Flores

All rights reserved. No part of this publication may be reproduced, distributed, or transmitted in any form or by any means, including photocopying, recording, or other electronic or mechanical methods, without the prior written permission of the publisher, except in the case of brief quotations embodied in critical reviews and certain other noncommercial uses permitted by copyright law.

TABLE OF CONTENTS

INTRODUCTION

CHAPTER ONE:

Getting to Know Riga

   About RIGA: Quick Facts and Statistics

   Geographical Overview

   Climate and Weather

   History and Culture

   Festivals and Events

CHAPTER TWO:

Planning Your Trip to Riga

   Best Time to Visit Riga

   Visa and Travel Requirements

   How to Get There

   Getting Around

   Accommodation Options

   Travel Insurance

CHAPTER THREE:

Exploring Riga's Top Attractions

   Riga Old Town

   Riga Central Market

   Art Nouveau District

   Riga Castle and National Museum of Latvia

   St. Peter's Church and Riga Cathedral

CHAPTER FOUR:

Uncovering Hidden Gems in Riga

   Riga Art Space

   Kalnciema Quarter

   Jurmala Beach

   Mezaparks

   Riga Motor Museum

CHAPTER FIVE:

Riga's Rich Cultural Heritage

   Latvian National Opera

   Riga's Art and History Museums

   Latvian Folklore and Traditions

Latvian Cuisine and Dining Experiences

Traditional Music and Dance

CHAPTER SIX:

Day Trips from Riga

- Sigulda and Gauja National Park
- Cesis Medieval Castle
- Jurmala Beach Resort
- Kemeri National Park
- Bauska Castle

CHAPTER SEVEN:

Exploring Riga's Neighborhoods

- Agenskalns
- Mezaparks
- Kipsala
- Vecriga (Old Town)
- Pardaugava

CHAPTER EIGHT:

Riga's Vibrant Nightlife

Bars and Pubs

Nightclubs and Lounges

Live Music Venues

Cultural Performances and Theater

Casinos and Gaming

CHAPTER NINE:
Riga's Culinary Delights

Latvian Traditional Dishes

International Cuisine

Local Food Markets and Street Food

Cafes and Bakeries

Craft Beer and Cocktail Bars

CHAPTER TEN:
Practical Information for Travelers

Transportation Options

Money and Currency Exchange

Language and Cultural Etiquette

Safety Tips and Emergency Contacts

Health and Medical Services

CHAPTER ELEVEN:

Shopping and Souvenirs in Riga

    Central Market and Shopping Centers

    Artisan Crafts and Souvenir Shops

    Latvian Amber and Jewelry

    Traditional Textiles and Woodwork

    Fashion and Design Boutiques

CHAPTER TWELVE:

Outdoor Adventures in Riga

    Parks and Gardens

    Riga Canal and Daugava River

    Cycling and Segway Tours

    Watersports and Sailing

    Winter Activities and Ice Skating

CHAPTER THIRTEEN:

Riga's Annual Events and Festivals:

    Riga City Festival

    Latvian Song and Dance Festival

    Riga Christmas Market

Summer Solstice Celebrations

International Music Festivals

CHAPTER FOURTEEN:

Riga for Art and History Lovers

  Art Galleries and Exhibitions

  Riga History Museums

  World War II History Sites

  Soviet Heritage and Architecture

  Riga's Art Nouveau Heritage

CHAPTER FIFTEEN:

Conclusion and Farewell to Riga

CHAPTER SIXTEEN:

Appendix

  30 Latvian Language Phrases with Pronunciations Guide

  Currency Conversion Chart

  Packing List for Riga

MAP OF RIGA

INTRODUCTION

Welcome to "Riga Vacation Guide 2023: The Essential and Ultimate Guide to Riga's Hotels, Cuisines, Shopping Tips, Insider's Tips, Top Attractions, History and Culture"! In the pages of this comprehensive guidebook, we invite you to embark on a remarkable journey through one of Europe's most captivating destinations – the magnificent city of Riga.

Riga, a city tucked away on the Baltic Sea coast, is a master at fusing the old with the contemporary. The Old Town, which is on the UNESCO World Heritage List, is a prime example of how its rich past coexists peacefully with a contemporary and international vibe. Riga guarantees every visitor an amazing vacation experience with its gorgeous architecture, fascinating cultural heritage, mouthwatering cuisine, and exciting nightlife.

We will introduce you to the best that Riga has to offer in 2023 as you turn the pages of this guide. Whether you are a seasoned tourist or a first-time visitor, our goal is to give you access to a thorough resource that will enable you to get the most out of your visit to this stunning Latvian city.

We start our journey by looking into the variety of lodging options available in Riga. We will assist you in choosing the ideal location to unwind and recharge after a day of discovering the city's treasures, from luxurious hotels with stunning views to inviting guesthouses that ooze local charm.

Without exploring the regional cuisine, no culinary journey is complete, and Riga is a culinary treasure just waiting to be found. We will tantalize your taste buds with a delectable assortment of traditional Latvian foods as well as a variety of other cuisines that have made a home in the city's burgeoning culinary scene.

The vibrant markets, chic boutiques, and cutting-edge shopping malls of Riga are heaven for shoppers. We will share the best shopping locations and insider insights to help you navigate the city's retail scene, which includes everything from high-end fashion and designer brands to traditional handicrafts and distinctive souvenirs.

Of course, no trip to Riga would be complete without taking in some of the city's major sights. We will lead you through the must-see attractions that characterize the character of the city, including the recognizable Art Nouveau architecture, the expansive Central Market, and the magnificent Riga Cathedral.

We will take you on a tour through Riga's interesting past as you immerse yourself in its dynamic present. Gain a deeper understanding of Riga's complicated and resilient history by learning the stories behind the city's historical sites, from the scars of Soviet control to the remains of the medieval Hanseatic League.

Riga has a thriving cultural environment that invites research beyond the obvious. We will open the doors to Riga's creative essence and provide insights into the city's cultural tapestry through world-class museums and art galleries, as well as exciting festivals and events.

"Riga Vacation Guide 2023" is your key to discovering the wonders of this magical city, whether you're a history buff, foodie, architecture enthusiast, or just a curious tourist looking for new experiences. Let us be your dependable guide while you explore Riga's streets, find hidden gems, and make lifelong memories.

Prepare yourself to encounter Riga's combination of history, culture, and unique adventures. Welcome to the starting point of your Riga vacation, the "Riga Vacation Guide 2023: The Essential and Ultimate Guide to Riga's Hotels, Cuisines, Shopping Tips, Insider's Tips, Top Attractions, History and Culture."

CHAPTER ONE:
Getting to Know Riga

About RIGA: Quick Facts and Statistics

Here are a few Riga-related fast facts and figures:

1. Population: With a population of roughly 632,000, Riga is the biggest city in Latvia. Additionally, it serves as the nation's political, economic, and cultural hub.

2. Language: The official language of Riga is Latvian. However, English is a common language in resort areas, hotels, and dining establishments.

3. Currency: The Euro (EUR) is the unit of currency in Riga.

4. Time Zone: Eastern European Time (EET), which is UTC+2 during standard time and UTC+3 during daylight saving time, is the time zone in which Riga is located.

5. UNESCO World Heritage Site: Known for its beautifully preserved medieval architecture and cobblestone alleys, Riga's Historic Center, usually referred to as the Old Town, is a UNESCO World Heritage site.

6. Architecture: The beautiful Art Nouveau architecture in Riga is well-known. It is home to one of the largest collections of Art Nouveau structures created by prominent architects including Mikhail Eisenstein and Konstantins Pkns.

7. Green Spaces: Riga is well-known for its many parks and green areas. The city has more than 30 parks, including the lovely Bastejkalns Park and the vast Meaparks, which provide locals and guests with tranquil sanctuaries inside the city.

8. Transportation: Riga has a reliable public transit network that includes buses, trams, and trolleybuses. These vehicles make it easy to go throughout the city. There are also lots of taxis and ride-sharing options.

9. Economy: With a broad economy that includes industries including finance, information technology, manufacturing, logistics, and tourism, Riga is a significant economic center in the Baltic area.

10. Education: The University of Latvia, Riga Technical University, and the Latvian Academy of Arts are just a few of the colleges and universities located in Riga.

11. Museums and Cultural Institutions: Riga is home to a thriving arts community that includes a wide array of museums and cultural organizations. The Latvian National Museum of Art, the Latvian Ethnographic Open-Air Museum, and the Museum of the Occupation of Latvia are a few noteworthy examples.

12. Sports: Ice hockey is among the most popular sports in Riga, which has a strong sports culture. The Riga Dinamo hockey team, a member of the Kontinental Hockey League (KHL), is based in the city.

These quick facts and statistics provide a glimpse into the vibrant and dynamic city of Riga, showcasing its cultural heritage, architectural splendor, and the many experiences it has to offer visitors.

Geographical Overview

Riga, the country's capital and largest city, is located on the Baltic Sea coast. At the mouth of the River Daugava, it holds a key position on the Gulf of Riga. The city is tucked away in the middle of the gorgeous landscape of forests, lakes, and rivers in Latvia's coastal plain. The approximate latitude and longitude of Riga are 56.95°N and 24.11°E, respectively.

Climate and Weather

A temperate coastal climate with considerable seasonal fluctuations prevails in Riga. The summer months of June through August are often cool and pleasant, with average highs and lows between 17°C and 22°C (63°F and 72°F). The best time of year to visit the city's outdoor attractions and take in its festivities. With temperatures averaging between

-5°C and 0°C (23°F and 32°F), the winter months of December through February can be chilly and snowy. Ice skating and other pleasant indoor activities are available as the city transforms into a winter paradise. The city is decorated with blossoming flowers in the spring and colorful fall foliage in the fall. Spring and autumn provide gentler weather.

History and Culture

The varied and rich history of Riga has influenced the city's distinct cultural identity. The German traders of the Livonian Order founded the city in the 12th century, when it became a major trading center. As a significant participant in the Hanseatic League, a medieval commercial organization, Riga prospered. The city has experienced the impact of numerous nations over the years, including Swedish, Polish, Russian, and German.

Riga's stunning architecture captures the city's historical significance. The Old Town, a UNESCO World Heritage site, displays an outstanding fusion of architectural styles, from magnificent Art Nouveau buildings to medieval constructions. Spires, domes, and elaborate facades decorate the city's skyline, giving a look into its extensive architectural history.

In Riga, there is a thriving and diverse cultural scene. The city is home to a large number of museums, galleries, and theaters that honor Latvian performing arts, art, and history. There is plenty to capture every creative taste, from classical concerts at the Latvian National Opera to contemporary exhibitions at the Art Museum Riga Bourse.

Festivals and Events

With a schedule bursting at the seams with exciting festivals and events, Riga comes alive all throughout the year. The Riga City Festival, which honors the city's founding every year in August, is among its highlights. It showcases the enthusiasm and creativity of Riga through a range of outdoor concerts, shows, fireworks, and parades.

The Staro Riga Light Festival, which takes place in November, transforms Riga's streets, buildings, and parks into a hypnotic visual extravaganza by illuminating the city with beautiful light installations and projections. This festival displays the inventiveness and artistic talent of the community.

The Riga Jurmala Music Festival, which takes place in the summer and features concerts by internationally famous orchestras and musicians in the picturesque settings of Riga and Jurmala, is a must-attend event for music lovers.

Other noteworthy occasions include the Christmas Market in December, where you can indulge in seasonal delights and peruse a variety of handmade products, and the Latvian Song and Dance Festival, a great celebration of traditional Latvian music and folk dance that takes place every five years.

These celebrations and activities make Riga a lively and exciting city all year long and offer a fascinating glimpse into Latvian customs, inventiveness, and cultural history.

Learning about Riga is a chance to explore a place with a rich past, a dynamic present, and a bright future. Travelers looking for an engaging and unforgettable experience will find it an enticing destination due to its stunning geographic location, varied climate, interesting history, and vibrant cultural scene.

CHAPTER TWO:
Planning Your Trip to Riga

Best Time to Visit Riga

Visiting Riga at the ideal moment can significantly improve your experience. The greatest time to visit depends on your tastes and interests because the city has something special to offer throughout the year.

In Riga, the summer (June to August) is the busiest travel period. With temperatures ranging from 17°C to 22°C (63°F to 72°F), the climate is comfortable, making it perfect for visiting outdoor sites and taking part in events. But around this time, expect bigger crowds and more expensive items.

In Riga, the shoulder seasons are spring (April to May) and fall (September to October). The pleasant weather and less busy city allow you to experience the attractions with less visitors. These are the best times of year to see Riga's stunning architecture, wander through the parks, and get to know the people.

Riga has a certain appeal during the winter (December to February). Snowy vistas and colorful accents turn the city into a winter wonderland. Visiting Riga in the winter can be a fantastic experience if you like ice skating and getting cozy in cafes. Winters can be chilly, with average temperatures ranging from -5°C to 0°C (23°F to 32°F), so keep that in mind.

Visa and Travel Requirements

Check the visa and travel requirements based on your nationality before making travel plans to Riga. Due to Latvia's membership in the European Union (EU) and the Schengen Area, many nationals, including those of the United States, Canada, Australia, and the majority of European nations, may travel there without a visa.

You must apply for a Schengen visa at the Latvian embassy or consulate in your home country if you are a citizen of a nation that needs a visa to enter the Schengen Zone. Check the precise requirements, such as the need for a valid passport, evidence of lodging, travel insurance, and enough money to cover your stay.

It is advisable to start the visa application process well in advance of your intended travel dates, as processing times may vary.

How to Get There

Travelers have a variety of alternatives because of the convenience of getting to Riga by air, land, and water.

- By Air: The main airport in the Baltic republics, Riga International Airport (RIX), acts as a significant hub for air travel to and from Riga. It provides a large number of flights linking Riga with numerous locations globally. Numerous significant airlines, notably the national airline of Latvia, Air Baltic, run frequent flights to Riga.

- By Land: Riga has efficient rail and road connections to its immediate neighbors. If you're coming from Europe, you may get to Riga by bus or train from places like Vilnius, Estonia; Tallinn, Lithuania; and Warsaw, Poland. The road system in Europe also makes it simple to drive to Riga.

- By Sea: Riga has a modern port that is a well-liked stop for cruise ships. On a Baltic cruise, you might dock in Riga and spend a day wandering around the city.

When making travel arrangements, take into account the modes of transportation that best match your tastes, spending limit, and schedule. To get the best offers and availability, it is important to reserve flights or other forms of transportation well in advance.

Getting Around

Once in Riga, there are many practical methods to navigate the area and take in its sights.

- Public Transportation: Buses, trams, and trolleybuses are all part of Riga's comprehensive and dependable public transit system. These transportation options cover the majority of the city and make it simple to get to different districts and sites. Either the driver or a ticket vending machine are options for purchasing tickets. It's worthwhile to think about getting a reusable e-ticket card, like the "e-talons," which provides lower rates for numerous trips.

- Taxis: In Riga, taxis are a practical and common form of transportation. You can utilize ride-hailing applications like Bolt or Red Cab or flag down a cab on the street. Use authorized taxi services, check if the meter is on, or negotiate a fare before the trip begins.

- Walking and Cycling: Riga is a great city to explore on foot because of its small size and protected medieval district. The majority of the major sights, businesses, eateries, and parks are close by and accessible on foot. Renting a bicycle is a terrific way to explore the city and take in its picturesque streets. Riga also boasts a growing network of cycling lanes.

Accommodation Options

Riga provides a variety of lodging choices to accommodate all tastes and price ranges.

- Hotels: There are many different hotels in the city, from high-end hotels to inexpensive alternatives. In Riga, there are numerous worldwide hotel brands offering up-to-date conveniences, cozy lodgings, and first-rate services. The city's core is where most hotels are located, especially in and around the Old Town and the neighboring Central District.

- Guesthouses and Hostels: Throughout Riga, guesthouses and hostels are available for those on a tight budget or those seeking a more sociable setting. These choices provide community areas, shared or private rooms, and the chance to socialize with other tourists. Some guesthouses are housed in old structures, which gives your stay a special character.

- Apartment Rentals: Renting an apartment or a vacation home might be a terrific choice for families or people who want more space and autonomy. You may experience Riga like a local by booking an apartment through one of the many platforms, like Booking.com and Airbnb.

Travel Insurance

Having travel insurance that covers lost luggage, medical crises, trip cancellations or interruptions, and other unforeseen events is highly advised. Travel insurance provides comfort and financial security in the event of any unforeseen circumstances while you are traveling.

Make sure you carefully research the coverage, policy limits, and exclusions before selecting travel insurance. Verify the insurance's coverage for medical costs, medical evacuation in case of emergency, and repatriation. Additionally, think about any particular hobbies or things you intend to take, and be sure the insurance coverage will cover them.

Before buying travel insurance, it is wise to speak with insurance providers, evaluate several plans, and choose the one that best meets your needs and offers sufficient protection for your trip to Riga.

You can effectively plan your trip and guarantee a smooth and enjoyable journey to this captivating city by taking into account the best time to visit, comprehending the visa and travel requirements, exploring the various options to reach Riga, exploring various accommodation options, and obtaining travel insurance.

CHAPTER THREE:
Exploring Riga's Top Attractions

With its extensive history and magnificent architecture, Riga has a wide range of top attractions that highlight the city's distinct character. Here are three places in Riga that you really must see:

Riga Old Town

A magnificent jewel of the city, Vecrga, or the Old Town of Riga, is a UNESCO World Heritage site. It attracts tourists because of its beautiful ambiance, Gothic architecture, and medieval streets. Romanesque, Gothic, Renaissance, and Baroque are just a few of the architectural styles you'll see as you stroll through the cobblestone streets.

The renowned Riga Cathedral, a majestic building from the 13th century, is located in Dome Square, the center of the Old Town. For sweeping views of the city, climb to the top of the cathedral's bell tower. The Swedish Gate, the House of the Blackheads, and St. Peter's Church are a few further Old Town highlights.

There are a ton of cafes, restaurants, boutiques, and gift shops in the Old Town. It's a great place to get to know the people and their culture, have some authentic Latvian food, and find one-of-a-kind crafts.

Riga Central Market

One of the biggest and liveliest markets in Europe, Riga Central Market is only a short stroll from the Old Town. The market, which is housed in five enormous zeppelin hangars, provides a sensory feast with its lively ambiance, vibrant vendors, and a variety of goods.

There are several different sections of the market, and each one offers a distinctive experience. Investigate the vegetable and fruit pavilion for a wide range of locally produced food. Explore the fish pavilion for a wide selection of fresh seafood and authentic Latvian smoked fish. Creamy cottage cheese and Latvian cheeses are among the dairy goods on display in the dairy pavilion.

The market sells household items, clothing, accessories, flowers, and food in addition to meals. It's a great spot to meet locals, take in Riga's dynamic energy, and eat some delectable Latvian cuisine.

Art Nouveau District

The Art Nouveau District in Riga is home to some of the best examples of Art Nouveau architecture anywhere in the world. Riga is known for its spectacular Art Nouveau architecture. The area around Alberta Street and Elizabetes Street (Alberta iela and Elizabetes iela) features a remarkable assortment of elaborate facades, detailed decorations, and decorative components.

Mikhail Eisenstein and Konstantins Pkns, two well-known Latvian architects, were responsible for the creation of several of the structures. Every turn is a visual spectacle because of the façade's beautiful sculptures, floral themes, and amusing figures.

Visit the Art Nouveau Museum, housed in a converted apartment, to learn more about the Art Nouveau style. The museum features items from the era's furniture and interior design. The museum sheds light on the artistic and cultural facets of Art Nouveau and its impact on the city of Riga's built environment.

You may enjoy the city's architectural legacy and learn more about Riga's contribution to the Art Nouveau movement by exploring the Art Nouveau District.

Riga Castle and National Museum of Latvia

Riga Castle is a famous landmark and the official house of the President of Latvia, perched on the banks of the Daugava River. The castle has a long and illustrious past that dates back to the 14th century, when the Livonian Order called it home. It experienced numerous architectural changes over the years, fusing features from the Gothic, Renaissance, and Baroque styles.

The National Museum of Latvia, which presents the history, art, and culture of the nation, is now located in Riga Castle. Artwork, historical records, archaeological objects, and ethnographic exhibits are all part of the museum's rich collection. It gives visitors a thorough grasp of Latvia's history, from its prehistoric origins to its contemporary evolution.

You may take a fascinating journey through Latvia's past by exploring Riga Castle and the National Museum of Latvia, and you can understand the significance of the castle as a marker of national identity.

St. Peter's Church and Riga Cathedral

One of Riga's most identifiable structures and a testament to the city's architectural prowess is St. Peter's Church. The church dominates the Old Town skyline with its enormous steeple. It was first constructed in the 13th century, but over time, it underwent various modifications and restorations.

When you visit St. Peter's Church, you may take in its impressive interior, which features ornate woodwork and stained-glass windows. Take a thrilling elevator journey to the viewing deck at the top of the church's spire for sweeping views of Riga. You can get breath-taking views of the city, the river, and further away from that point.

Another major place of worship and architectural significance is the Riga Cathedral, also referred to as the Riga Dom. The 13th century saw the construction of one of the largest medieval churches in the Baltic republics. The spectacular interior of the cathedral has stunning stained glass windows, a powerful organ, and complex stone and wood carvings.

The cathedral contains a number of noteworthy features, such as the historic 19th-century organ and the medieval baptismal font, both of which are known for their outstanding acoustics. The Museum of the History of Riga and Navigation, which is located inside the cathedral, features exhibits on the cathedral's construction as well as information about the city's nautical past.

Riga Cathedral and St. Peter's Church both provide insights into the city's opulent architectural history. They are required stops for anybody interested in the city's rich history and creative accomplishments because of their historical and cultural significance.

When you visit these sites, you can not only appreciate their stunning architecture but also learn about the rich cultural and historical background of Riga. Riga's main attractions, which range from castles, markets, and cathedrals to museums and churches, provide a variety of experiences that cater to a variety of interests and leave tourists with enduring memories of this alluring Baltic city.

CHAPTER FOUR:
Uncovering Hidden Gems in Riga

Although Riga's main attractions are well-known and frequently visited, the city also contains a number of undiscovered treasures that provide a more unique experience. These three obscure sites are worthwhile exploring:

Riga Art Space

In the center of the city is the contemporary art gallery known as Riga Art Space. This undiscovered treasure, tucked away from the main tourist attractions, presents a variety of exhibitions of modern and contemporary art. The gallery, located in a converted warehouse, offers artists a distinctive and immersive space to present their work.

Painting, sculpture, photography, and multimedia installations are just a few of the creative disciplines represented in the recurring exhibitions at Riga creative Space. The gallery actively supports regional and worldwide artists, providing visitors with the opportunity to view cutting-edge and provocative contemporary art.

Riga Art Space is a lively center for art lovers because it organizes talks, workshops, and activities pertaining to art in addition to exhibitions. You may immerse yourself in Riga's vibrant art scene and learn about up-and-coming artists by unearthing this hidden gem.

Kalnciema Quarter

Just outside the city center is the restored Kalnciema Quarter, which offers a lovely and peaceful retreat from Riga's busy streets. With its collection of wonderfully preserved wooden structures and cobblestone streets, this hidden gem evokes memories of bygone eras.

A weekly market where local farmers and artists come together to sell their wares is one of the many activities held in the district. The market features a diverse selection of handmade goods, organic foods, traditional crafts, and live musical acts. It's the ideal chance to meet people, indulge in delectable cuisine, and buy interesting trinkets.

The Kalnciema Quarter also has cafes, art galleries, stores, and a cultural center in addition to the market. It serves as a focal point for artistic endeavors, social gatherings, and cultural activities like performances, exhibits, and festivals. You may discover Riga's true charm and see how dedicated the city is to maintaining its cultural legacy by exploring this hidden gem.

Jurmala Beach

Jurmala, an undiscovered gem on the Baltic Sea shore, is located not far from Riga. This resort community is well-known for its picturesque dunes, sand beaches, and calm atmosphere that provide a soothing getaway from the city.

Over 30 kilometers of Jurmala Beach offer plenty of room to relax, enjoy the sun, and take energizing water dips. A promenade lined with quaint hotels, wooden homes, and comfortable cafes complements the beach. It's the ideal location for taking a leisurely stroll, taking in the breathtaking sea views, and indulging in delectable seaside fare.

Beyond the beach, Jurmala provides a range of leisure pursuits, such as horseback riding, biking, and nature hikes in the nearby Kemeri National Park. The town also holds a number of cultural events, including festivals, concerts, and art exhibitions, which highlight the local talent and liven up the tranquil coastal ambiance.

Discovering Jurmala Beach's hidden charm enables you to experience the calm and natural beauty of the Baltic Sea shoreline while also relaxing and exploring.

Mezaparks

Mezaparks, a lush district in the northern part of Riga, is a tranquil haven away from the city's bustle. The rich vegetation, serene lakes, and recreational options of this hidden gem are well-known.

One of Mezaparks' features is its sizable park, which is one of Riga's biggest and most beautiful parks and covers more than 265 hectares. The park is the ideal setting for leisurely strolls, picnics, or bike rides thanks to its winding trails, picturesque surroundings, and plenty of flora and fauna.

The lovely Kisezers Lake is located within Mezaparks, where you may go boating, fishing, or just relax and take in the scenery. Forested areas surround the lake, enhancing the area's natural attractiveness.

Mezaparks is also the location of a number of attractions, such as the Mezaparks Open-Air Stage. Summertime brings a variety of cultural events and music festivals to this outdoor concert venue. A live concert at the Mezaparks Open-Air Stage gives you the chance to take in music in a gorgeous environment amidst nature.

Mezaparks is also renowned for its stunning wooden villas and Art Nouveau-style homes. These unique buildings give the area charm and personality while offering a window into the city's architectural past.

Riga Motor Museum

The Riga Motor Museum is a well-kept secret that takes visitors on an enthralling tour through the development of transportation. This museum, which is not far from the city center, features an excellent collection of classic cars, motorcycles, and other automobiles.

The museum's exhibits showcase well-known automobile brands and types from a variety of eras, including early horse-drawn carriages, vintage cars from the 20th century, and even automobiles from the Soviet era. Visitors can learn about the advancements in automobile technology and design through the collection and understand how transportation has changed over time.

The Riga Motor Museum not only has a large collection of automobiles, but it also has engaging exhibits, multimedia shows, and interactive displays that explore the history of the vehicles and their influence on society. Visitors can discover the history of the automotive industry's pioneers, investigate the cultural relevance of autos, and be in awe of historical engineering feats.

The museum offers engaging experiences for visitors of all ages by hosting temporary exhibitions, special events, and educational programs. The Riga Motor Museum is a hidden gem that provides a memorable and instructive experience, whether you're an automobile aficionado or are just interested in the evolution of transportation.

It is possible to gain a greater appreciation for Riga's aesthetic, cultural, and ecological attractions by exploring these hidden gems. The nostalgic allure of

Kalnciema Quarter, the tranquil beaches of Jurmala, or the contemporary art at Riga Art Space—these hidden jewels offer a dimension of discovery and enchantment to your trip to Riga.

Unique and less well-known sights like Mezaparks and the Riga Motor Museum offer a change of pace from the usual tourist destinations. These undiscovered gems in Riga provide an educational and unforgettable experience, whether you're looking for peace in nature or an investigation into the history of the automobile.

CHAPTER FIVE:
Riga's Rich Cultural Heritage

The capital of Latvia, Riga, has a long history and a rich cultural heritage. Riga provides a wide variety of cultural events, from its world-famous opera theater and art museums to its rich folklore and culinary traditions. Here are a few of the highlights:

Latvian National Opera

At the center of Riga's cultural landscape lies the Latvian National Opera. The opera, ballet, and classical music concerts are held in this majestic neoclassical structure all year long.

The Latvian National Opera offers a unique performance experience that highlights the skills and artistry of regional performers. The opera theater has a varied schedule that appeals to a variety of creative inclinations, from top-notch opera productions to enthralling ballet performances.

Riga's Art and History Museums

The excellent collection of art and history museums in Riga offers insights into the city's rich cultural past. A large collection of Latvian and foreign artwork, including traditional and contemporary works, is housed in the Latvian National Museum of Art, which is housed in a remarkable Art Nouveau structure.

In order to provide a thorough understanding of the nation's challenges and resiliency, the Museum of the Occupation of Latvia documents Latvia's history during the Soviet and Nazi occupations. The Museum of Decorative Arts and Design, the Museum of the History of Riga and Navigation, and other noteworthy museums include the Riga History and Navigation Museum.

These museums give visitors a look at Riga's past, creative accomplishments, and societal developments that have molded the city over time.

Latvian Folklore and Traditions

The traditions and folklore of Latvia are fundamental to the culture of the nation. Mythical stories, folk music (dainas), traditional clothing, and handicrafts are also part of the extensive folklore. Knowledge of Latvian folklore helps one have a better knowledge of the country's ties to the natural world, its agricultural heritage, and its sense of community.

Every year, a variety of cultural gatherings and festivals honor Latvian folklore. Every five years, thousands of performers showcase traditional music, dance, and choral singing during the Latvian Song and Dance Celebration. Other celebrations, like Midsummer (Ji) and the Riga City Festival, promote the traditions, music, and cuisine of Latvia.

Latvian Cuisine and Dining Experiences

Latvian food is a delicious representation of the nation's natural resources, seasonal ingredients, and traditional culinary techniques. You may try traditional Latvian cuisine in Riga at a variety of restaurants and learn about the city's culinary culture.

Grey peas with bacon, potato pancakes, sauerkraut, and smoked fish are just a few examples of the substantial and satisfying foods found in traditional Latvian cuisine. A mainstay of the diet is "rupjmaize," or Latvian rye bread. In addition, native foods like honey, berries, and mushrooms are favorites of Latvians.

You may eat at a variety of establishments in Riga, from quaint taverns selling traditional fare to cutting-edge restaurants giving creative takes on Latvian cuisine. You can experience Latvian delicacies and gain an appreciation for the nation's culinary legacy by learning more about the culinary scene in Riga.

Traditional Music and Dance

The colorful representations of the nation's cultural heritage that are traditional music and dance in Latvia. Choral singing is highly regarded in Latvia and is an important part of their cultural heritage. The force of group singing and the beauty of classic Latvian music are both on display during the aforementioned Latvian Song and Dance Celebration.

Another fascinating feature of Latvia's cultural history is its folk dances, which are frequently accompanied by live music. These dances have complex footwork, upbeat music, and colorful costumes. The fire and grace of Latvian folk dance are on display throughout the year at performances by traditional dance groups and ensembles.

You can become completely engrossed in the rhythmic melodies and the vivacious atmosphere that are strongly embedded in Latvian culture by taking part in a traditional music or dance event in Riga.

The diverse creative forms, customs, and gastronomic delicacies that make up Riga's rich cultural legacy are numerous. Riga offers a wide range of cultural experiences that leave an enduring impression on visitors, including attending opera performances at the Latvian National Opera, exploring the city's art and history museums, embracing Latvian folklore and traditions, savoring traditional cuisine, and experiencing the joy of traditional music and dance.

CHAPTER SIX:
Day Trips from Riga

Riga is a great place to start seeing Latvia's historical and natural attractions because of its central location. These three intriguing day trips from Riga provide a range of experiences:

Sigulda and Gauja National Park

Sigulda and Gauja National Park appeal with their gorgeous scenery and medieval charm just one hour's drive from Riga. The largest national park in Latvia, Gauja National Park, is known as the "Latvian Switzerland" for its breathtaking beauty.

The lovely village of Sigulda, also known as the "Latvian Switzerland," is located in the Gauja River Valley. The town is well-known for its historical sites, beautiful scenery, and outdoor pursuits. One of the attractions is the impressive red-brick stronghold from the 13th century known as Sigulda Castle. Visitors can stroll along the castle's walls, explore the remains, and take in expansive views of the surrounding landscape.

The Turaida Castle, which is close by and another must-see destination in Sigulda, is also nearby. In addition to providing a window into the past, this well-preserved medieval castle includes a picturesque tower climb that rewards climbers with stunning vistas.

Gauja National Park, with its thick forests, sandstone cliffs, and flowing rivers, offers lots of activities for nature lovers. The park is filled with hiking routes that take you to picturesque locations like the Gutmanis Cave, a historic and culturally significant location with inscriptions from the 17th century.

Visitors seeking an adrenaline rush can try bobsledding on the Sigulda bobsleigh course, which is open all year and offers a distinctive and exhilarating experience.

Cesis Medieval Castle

About one and a half hours from Riga is Cesis, a lovely town with a well-preserved medieval core. The Cesis Medieval Castle, which dates to the 13th century, is the town's main attraction.

Ruins of the castle are positioned atop a hill, offering a mesmerizing view of the surroundings. The castle grounds' old walls, turrets, and courtyards transport visitors back in time as they evoke the opulence of the Middle Ages.

With its historic structures, charming gardens, and cobblestoned streets, Cesis is a delightful town to explore. The town's distinctive and enchanted environment is a result of the medieval feel blended with its contemporary cultural activities and festivals.

Jurmala Beach Resort

Jurmala, a well-liked seaside resort town with lovely sand beaches, pine trees, and elegant wooden buildings, is only 30 minutes' drive from Riga.

The 26-kilometer-long stretch of sandy beaches along the Baltic Sea is Jurmala's primary draw. Visitors can unwind on the beach, cool off in the sea, or engage in a variety of water sports and activities.

The town's wooden construction, especially in the region referred to as the "Jurmala Open-Air

Museum," displays the attractive and distinctive design of traditional Latvian coastal cottages. With its lively ambiance, charming cafes, and gift shops, Jomas Street, the major pedestrian thoroughfare, is a pleasant experience to stroll along.

Beyond its beaches and landmarks, Jurmala hosts concerts, art exhibits, and cultural events during the summer, giving the area a more creative feel.

Kemeri National Park

A nature lover's heaven, Kemeri National Park is about an hour's drive west of Riga. Its natural forests, marshes, lakes, and coastal vistas define this huge and varied park.

The Kemeri Bog Boardwalk, a wooden walkway that meanders through the scenic marshes, is a famous feature of the park. Visitors can view the area's distinctive flora and fauna, including rare plant species and diverse bird species, while strolling along the boardwalk. It's the ideal location for relaxation and nature photography because of the serene ambiance and breathtaking views.

In addition, Kemeri National Park has a network of hiking paths that take visitors to undiscovered attractions like the Great Emeri Bog and Lake Kaieris. These routes offer chances to explore the park's various ecosystems, find undiscovered lakes, and take in the tranquility of nature.

The therapeutic mud baths and mineral-rich thermal springs at Kemeri National Park are well-known in addition to its natural marvels. Visitors can indulge in health pursuits like mineral baths and mud treatments, which are thought to have therapeutic benefits for the skin and body.

Bauska Castle

A historical treasure that provides a window into medieval Latvia is Bauska Castle, which is roughly an hour's drive south of Riga. The Renaissance palace and the medieval fortress make up the entire castle complex.

Built in the 15th century as a defensive bastion, the medieval fortification known as the Old Castle is also known as. Visitors can imagine the castle's past splendor and get knowledge of its strategic importance in the area by exploring its ruins.

A pedestrian bridge links the majestic Renaissance-style palace known as the New Castle to the Old Castle. The architectural and aesthetic influences of the era are on display in this area of the complex. You can go inside to the museum, which displays historical objects and provides information about the history of the castle and the local cultural heritage.

The Msa and Mmele rivers' confluence is visible from the castle's tower, which also offers sweeping views of the surrounding countryside. History buffs and lovers of architecture go to the castle because of its picturesque location and historical relevance.

When you go to Bauska Castle, you may learn about Latvia's medieval past, see the architectural wonders of the castle complex, and take in the surrounding area's stunning scenery.

When you take a day excursion from the busy metropolis of Riga, you may explore Latvia's natural beauty, medieval history, and seaside appeal at Sigulda and Gauja National Park, Cesis Medieval Castle, or Jurmala Beach Resort. These day trips offer a lovely retreat, whether your interests include discovering historic castles, experiencing nature firsthand, or simply unwinding by the sea.

Additionally, the Kemeri National Park and Bauska Castle provide singular and educational experiences that highlight Latvia's various topographies, historical legacy, and natural beauties. These locations offer a pleasant overview of the country outside of Riga, whether you're looking for outdoor adventures, historical beauty, or peaceful nature escapes.

CHAPTER SEVEN:
Exploring Riga's Neighborhoods

The vivacious capital of Latvia, Riga, is a diversified metropolis with a range of neighborhoods, each of which offers its own charm and personality. Let's examine five illustrious areas that are worth visiting:

Agenskalns

Just west of the city center of Riga, on the left bank of the Daugava River, is the historic district of Agenskalns. This neighborhood is well-known for its charming wooden houses, tree-lined lanes, and laid-back vibe.

The neighborhood's architecture is a synthesis of several different architectural eras, including Art Nouveau, wooden Jugendstil, and traditional timber dwellings. It's a lovely place to stroll through and perfectly captures Riga's architectural history.

A rich cultural environment is another strength of Agenskalns. An active center for culture and entertainment has emerged from the once-industrial Spikeri Creative Quarter. It features a variety of activities, including concerts, art exhibitions, and fashionable cafes and eateries. The area's redevelopment demonstrates Riga's dedication to maintaining its historic charm while embracing contemporary ingenuity.

Mezaparks

On Riga's northeastern outskirts, Mezaparks is a lush green haven. This area is known for its vast parkland, calm lakes, and stunning villas in the Art Nouveau style.

The name-brand park, which covers more than 270 hectares and provides a wide range of recreational opportunities, is the focal point of Mezaparks. It is the location of the Riga Zoo, where you may learn about a variety of animal species. The Mezaparks Open-Air Stage, a well-liked music venue where outdoor performances and festivals take place during the summer, is another attraction in the park along with walking and cycling routes, picnic spots, and playgrounds.

Mezaparks offers chances for leisurely strolls, bike rides, or just taking in the peace and quiet of the surrounding vegetation, making it the perfect getaway for nature enthusiasts.

Kipsala

Just a short distance from Riga's city center is the scenic island community of Kipsala, which is located on the Daugava River. Kipsala, which is connected to the mainland by a bridge, is renowned for its quaint wooden buildings, cutting-edge housing projects, and a bohemian vibe.

The area offers breathtaking waterfront views as well as a marina where you may gaze at yachts and boats. The Kipsala International Exhibition Centre, which holds a variety of trade fairs, conferences, and cultural events all year long, is also located in Kipsala.

Kipsala is a popular residential area and a fun area to visit due to its close proximity to the city center and distinctive fusion of traditional and modern architecture.

Vecriga (Old Town)

Vecriga, commonly referred to as the Old Town of Riga, is the city's historic core and a UNESCO World Heritage site. This area is a fascinating blend of winding cobblestone alleyways, historic structures, and exciting cultural attractions.

The Riga Cathedral, St. Peter's Church, and the House of the Blackheads are among the well-known attractions of Vecriga. The Gothic, Renaissance, and Baroque architectural influences in the area combine to produce an aesthetically spectacular atmosphere.

The area is also a thriving center for eateries, cafes, bars, and shops, providing a lively ambiance day and night. You may learn about Vecriga's fascinating history, visit museums and art galleries, and take in the exciting street performances that frequently take place in the city's prominent squares by strolling through the city's twisting streets.

Pardaugava

The communities on the right bank of the Daugava River are known as Pardaugava, which translates to "across the Daugava." This region offers a blend of residential, commercial, and cultural venues and offers a new perspective on Riga.

The architecture in Pardaugava is varied and includes both contemporary constructions and apartment buildings from the Soviet era. The National Library of Latvia, sometimes known as the "Castle of Light," is a spectacular glass and steel structure that is one of the area's most well-known attractions.

The Andrejsala neighborhood, a hub for the arts and creative endeavors, is also part of the Pardaugava neighborhood. It has repurposed industrial and warehouse structures that contain art studios, galleries, and cultural events. Andrejsala is a hidden gem where you may discover modern art, see exhibitions, and interact with the neighborhood's creative scene.

Discovering Riga's neighborhoods, such as Agenskalns, Mezaparks, Kipsala, Vecriga, and Pardaugava, provides a comprehensive picture of the city's past, architectural variety, cultural vibrancy, and natural beauty. Each district in Riga has a unique personality that allows tourists to learn more about the city's rich tapestry.

CHAPTER EIGHT:
Riga's Vibrant Nightlife

If you're searching for a quaint bar to unwind in, a buzzing nightclub to dance the night away in, or a place to catch live music performances, Riga's nightlife culture has something for everyone. Let's investigate the various aspects of Riga's nightlife:

Bars and Pubs

There are numerous bars and pubs in Riga that provide something for everyone. You'll discover a variety of options to suit your tastes, from hip cocktail lounges to classic Latvian beer taverns.

The Old Town is a well-known destination for taverns and pubs because of its cozy ambience and avenues dotted with establishments. From cozy wine bars with wide drink selections to craft beer pubs serving a variety of domestic and foreign brews, you can find it all here.

Another popular destination for distinctive bars is Miera iela in Riga's alternative neighborhood. This street is well-known for its bohemian atmosphere and has a variety of hipster bars where you can unwind with artisan beers, inventive drinks, and live music.

Nightclubs and Lounges

The nightlife in Riga is thriving, with a wide variety of nightclubs and lounges that appeal to aficionados of electronic music, popular music, and upscale settings.

In the middle of Riga, particularly in the Terbatas Street and Livu Square neighborhoods, is where the city's clubbing hotspot is located. Here, you'll find sizable clubs with well-known DJs, outstanding sound systems, and enthralling lighting designs that produce an electric environment.

Riga has a variety of lounges and rooftop bars where you can enjoy panoramic views of the city skyline and artisan drinks if you want a more upscale and sophisticated atmosphere. These places frequently offer themed gatherings, live DJ performances, or even special guest appearances by foreign performers.

Live Music Venues

Riga provides a variety of live music venues where music lovers can take in performances in a variety of genres, including jazz, rock, pop, and traditional Latvian music.

Concert halls in Riga, like the Great Guild and the Palladium, welcome both regional and foreign performers, presenting a wide variety of musical skills. These locations host numerous concerts, festivals, and special events all year long, making them a mecca for music enthusiasts.

Riga has smaller, more private venues that offer a warm environment for live music performances in addition to concert halls. Jazz clubs, like the well-known Trompete and Kaepes Culture Center, offer evenings full of improvised music and passionate songs. These places frequently feature great local musicians and offer jam sessions.

The lively street music culture in Riga also contributes to the musical atmosphere of the city. During the summer, you're likely to come across street performers and buskers filling the air with beautiful tunes as you stroll around the Old Town or central squares.

Cultural Performances and Theater

Bars, clubs, and live music venues are only a small part of Riga's nightlife. The city is also home to a bustling cultural scene that presents a variety of theatrical productions and shows.

A notable venue that presents opera, ballet, and classical music events is the Latvian National Opera. It is housed in a stunning old building in the heart of the city and presents top-notch shows with gifted performers from all over the world, including Latvia.

There are several theaters in Riga that offer a range of theatrical productions, from modern plays to classics. Among the major theaters where you can see engaging performances by gifted actors and actresses are the Dailes Theatre and the National Theatre.

Along with conventional theater, Riga supports unconventional and experimental performing arts. Innovative and thought-provoking performances that go beyond the bounds of conventional stage productions are presented by experimental theater companies and independent performing arts venues.

You can feel the aesthetic and intellectual atmosphere of the city and the creative energy that permeates its cultural institutions by going to a cultural performance or theater production in Riga.

Casinos and Gaming

Riga has a variety of casinos and gaming businesses for people looking for a little excitement and amusement.

From traditional table games like blackjack, roulette, and poker to a multitude of slot machines and electronic gaming options, the city's casinos cater to a wide spectrum of interests. The biggest casinos are frequently found inside of hotels and entertainment hubs and provide a wide range of amenities and services.

The busiest gambling district in Riga is located in the city's heart, mainly around Terbatas and Elizabetes Streets. With colorful lights, upbeat music, and the opportunity to try your luck at the gaming tables, these businesses offer a sophisticated and vivacious ambiance.

It's important to keep in mind that Riga's casinos frequently offer special occasions, such as poker tournaments or themed parties, which up the excitement level of the gaming experience.

The vibrant and friendly environment of Riga's nightlife is well-known. It's crucial to remember that weekends are typically the liveliest, with both residents and visitors swarming the city's venues. Every night owl can find something to do in Riga's dynamic nightlife, whether they want to dance till morning, unwind with a drink in a welcoming pub, or take in live music performances.

CHAPTER NINE:
Riga's Culinary Delights

With its diversified culinary scene, the city of Riga tempts the taste buds. Riga provides a vast variety of gastronomic delights to please every palate, from delicious street food to bustling food markets, from traditional Latvian delicacies to foreign cuisine. Let's delve deeper into these culinary highlights:

Latvian Traditional Dishes

Latvia's rich cultural legacy and natural resources are reflected in its cuisine. Grains, potatoes, fish, meat, dairy products, and wild fruits are among the locally sourced components frequently used in traditional Latvian recipes. These Latvian delicacies are a must-try:

- Rupjmaize: A mainstay of Latvian cuisine, this dark rye bread. It tastes slightly sweet and sour and has a solid texture. Common toppings include cheese, butter, and other ingredients.

- Pelmeni: These little dumplings are served with sour cream and minced meat, typically pork. In Latvia, they are a well-liked comfort dish.

- Skābeņu zupa: Made from the tart sorrel plant leaves, this traditional Latvian soup is also known as sorrel soup. It is frequently served with boiled eggs, potatoes, and sour cream on the side.

- Pīrāgi: These delectable Latvian pastries resemble pierogies or stuffed buns. They typically contain bacon and onions, making them a flavorful and filling snack.

International Cuisine

Latvian cuisine is just one aspect of Riga's gastronomic landscape. The city embraces global cuisine, and there are a wide variety of restaurants and cafés serving food from all over the world. Riga can satisfy your cravings for American-style hamburgers, Asian fusion, Middle Eastern cuisine, or Italian pasta.

International eateries congregate around the city center, especially in the Old Town and adjacent neighborhoods. Here, you'll discover upmarket restaurants, quaint bistros, and hip cafes, each of which offers a distinctive gastronomic experience.

To meet the rising demand for plant-based meals, Riga also has an expanding number of vegetarian and vegan eateries. These restaurants provide imaginative, tasty cuisine that emphasize the abundance of local, fresh vegetables.

Local Food Markets and Street Food

Visit the neighborhood markets for a taste of Riga's thriving food culture. One of Europe's biggest and most stunning markets is the centrally positioned Riga Central Market. It sells a huge variety of fresh vegetables, meat, seafood, dairy products, baked foods, and other items out of old zeppelin hangars.

As citizens congregate to purchase for their daily necessities, you may observe the bustle of city life by exploring Riga Central Market. Within the market, there are also a number of modest eateries where you may sample foods and snacks that are uniquely Latvian.

The street food scene in Riga is also well-known. Food trucks and kiosks selling a variety of delicious foods fill the city's streets and squares. Street food in Riga is a fantastic opportunity to sample regional flavors while on the road, offering anything from delectable kebabs and grilled sausages to sweet pastries and freshly brewed coffee.

Additionally, throughout the year, Riga holds a number of food festivals where you may experience a wide range of foods, including both traditional Latvian food and cuisine from other countries.

Cafes and Bakeries

With its countless lovely cafes and bakeries strewn all over the city, Riga is a sanctuary for coffee aficionados. These businesses offer wonderful cups of coffee in addition to a welcoming setting where customers may unwind and indulge in sweets.

Several well-known bakeries and cafes in Riga include:

- MiiT Coffee: Popular with both locals and tourists, MiiT Coffee is known for its specialty coffee and laid-back atmosphere. You can have finely made coffees here, such as pour-overs and espresso-based drinks, along with a variety of recently baked pastries.

- Riga Black Balsam Cafe: This Old Town café is well-known for its inventive take on the classic Latvian liquor Black Balsam. Enjoy a cup of coffee flavored with Black Balsam, or try some of their sweets and chocolates that have been flavored with this unique herbal liqueur.

- Martins Dukurs Bakery: A hidden gem in Riga, this artisan bakery serves a variety of freshly made bread, pastries, and cakes. They provide scrumptious

European-style pastries in addition to traditional Latvian pastries like biezpienmaize (curd pastry) and kartupelu pankkas (potato pancakes).

Craft Beer and Cocktail Bars

Additionally, the emerging craft beer and cocktail scenes in Riga have attracted attention. Craft beer lovers can choose from a vast variety of domestic and foreign craft brews at the many bars and breweries that are available. The following Riga establishments serve craft beer:

-Alus Celle: Situated in the center of the Old Town, Alus Celle is a welcoming tavern with a wide variety of artisan beers on tap. The educated staff can help you through their large menu, which offers a range of styles and flavors to satisfy the tastes of all beer connoisseurs.

- Labietis: This avant-garde brewery and taproom is committed to creating one-of-a-kind, experimental beers utilizing ingredients that are found locally. Labietis offers a genuinely unique beer-drinking experience with a constantly changing assortment of beers available on tap.

Riga is home to a thriving bar culture that offers a wide variety of cocktails. You can choose from a wide range of establishments that serve beautifully created cocktails made with premium alcohol and seasonal ingredients, from vintage cocktail lounges to hip mixology bars. Some well-known cocktail bars in Riga are:

- Vest: This chic cocktail establishment in the center of the city is renowned for its creative concoctions. The Vest bartenders are enthusiastic about mixology and work hard to develop distinctive flavor combinations that please customers.

- Aperitivo: This quaint, small pub specializes in aperitifs and traditional cocktails. Aperitivo is the ideal location for relaxing and savoring a well-made cocktail because of its welcoming and pleasant ambiance.

In conclusion, the culinary scene in Riga is a veritable storehouse of tastes and adventures. Riga provides a gourmet trip that is certain to create a lasting impression, whether you are indulging in traditional Latvian foods, discovering exotic cuisines, or engrossing yourself in the lively ambiance of local food markets and street food. Additionally, Riga's cafés, bakeries, craft beer bars, and cocktail lounges offer a fascinating voyage for your taste buds whether you're looking for a caffeine fix, discovering the world of craft beer, or indulging in perfectly made cocktails.

CHAPTER TEN:
Practical Information for Travelers

Transportation Options

Riga has a good transit system, making getting around the city simple. Here are a few choices for getting around during your visit:

- Public Transportation: There is a comprehensive network of buses, trams, and trolleybuses in Riga. Travelers can easily tour various neighborhoods and attractions because the public transit system serves the entire city and its environs. Kiosks, ticket machines, and the driver themselves all offer the option of purchasing tickets.

- Taxis: You may either order a cab through a taxi app or hail one on the street in Riga. Use trustworthy taxi services or negotiate the fee with the driver before setting out on your route.

- Bike Rental: The city of Riga has a system for sharing bicycles called "Riga Bike," which enables you to borrow a bike for a short time. This is a fantastic way to discover the parks and bike-friendly regions of the city.

Money and Currency Exchange

The Euro (EUR) is the country of Latvia's official currency. The following advice is for money and currency conversion in Riga:

- Currency Exchange: There are several currency exchange offices in Riga, especially in popular tourist districts and at the airport. Before engaging in a transaction, it is advisable to compare currency rates and costs. In addition, banks offer currency exchange services throughout regular business hours.

- Credit Cards and ATMs: Hotels, restaurants, and other major enterprises accept credit cards widely. Nevertheless, it's wise to always have some cash on hand for smaller businesses and neighborhood markets. The city is filled with ATMs where you may get cash in the local currency.

- Tipping: Tipping is appreciated but not required in Riga. If you're happy with the service, it's traditional to round up the amount or give a 5–10% tip.

Language and Cultural Etiquette

You can have a much better time in Riga if you are aware of the local language and customs. To remember, have the following in mind:

- Language: Latvia's official tongue is Latvian. Although many people in Riga speak English, particularly in tourist areas, hotels, and restaurants, Latvian is a common language, especially among older generations. To respect and interact with the local culture, it can be beneficial to learn a few simple Latvian phrases.

- Cultural Etiquette: In general, Latvians are amiable and inviting. It is polite to provide a firm handshake and make eye contact while greeting someone. It's crucial to be on time for appointments and meetings because punctuality is highly regarded. When entering someone's home, you should also take off your shoes out of respect.

- Dress Code: Riga has a generally informal dress code, while some places could have a more formal dress code. When going to fancy restaurants or holy institutions, it is best to dress accordingly.

- Respect for Nature and the Environment: Latvia is proud of its natural beauty, therefore it's crucial to respect and protect it while you're there. Keeping to defined trails in parks and natural reserves, not littering, and abiding by any rules or restrictions set forth at protected areas are examples of this.

Safety Tips and Emergency Contacts

It is crucial to ensure your safety while going through Riga. Here are some current safety recommendations and emergency numbers to remember:

- Stay Vigilant: Riga is typically a safe city, but it's always vital to be alert, especially in congested places and popular tourist destinations. Keep an eye on your possessions, don't flaunt pricey stuff, and be wary of pickpockets. Keep an eye on your surroundings and believe in your gut.

- Emergency Contacts: Keep in mind the following numbers in case of emergencies:
  - Police: 112 (general emergency number)
  - Ambulance: 113
  - Fire Department: 112

- Travel Insurance: Having travel insurance that pays for medical costs, trip cancellation or interruption, and personal responsibility is strongly advised. Before your travel, be sure to review your insurance and comprehend the coverage.

- Secure Accommodation: Pick trustworthy lodging options with secure access, and think about using security features like hotel safes to protect your priceless possessions.

- Transportation Safety: Use authorized taxis or trustworthy ride-sharing services to ensure your safety when traveling. If you intend to go by public transit, take extra care with your possessions and keep an eye out for any rumors of scams or unlicensed ticket vendors.

- Be Mindful of Scams: destination, there can be those seeking to con or dupe tourists. Avoid unwanted offers, excessively nice strangers, and never rely solely on information from unreliable sources.

Health and Medical Services

Both public and private medical facilities are available in Riga, which offers high-quality healthcare services. Here are some crucial details about Riga's health and medical systems:

- Health Insurance: Make sure you have complete travel health insurance that pays for medical costs, emergency medical evacuation, and repatriation.

- Vaccinations: Before visiting Riga, confirm the most recent advice from your nation's health agency or speak with a medical expert regarding any necessary or advised vaccinations.

- Pharmacies: Pharmacies, or aptieka in Latvian, are present all across Riga. Most pharmacies are open during typical business hours, while others could be open around-the-clock. It is advisable to bring a modest supply of any prescription medication you need, as well as a formal prescription or other supporting documentation.

- Emergency Medical Services: Dial 113 to request an ambulance in the event of a medical emergency. In Riga, the emergency services are prepared and quick to act.

- Language Barrier: The majority of people in hospitals and clinics, especially those with bigger patient populations, speak English. However, it is advised to have access to translation services if necessary or to carry a copy of vital medical records that have been translated into English.

- Traveler's Health Precautions: To avoid contracting any foodborne illnesses while traveling, it is crucial to exercise good hygiene habits including often washing your hands, drinking bottled or treated water, and being cautious while eating street food.

Prior to your journey to Riga, it is essential to speak with your doctor or a travel medicine expert to receive individualized suggestions based on your medical history and unique requirements.

You can move around Riga with ease and respect for local customs by becoming familiar with the city's transportation options, learning about its financial system, being aware of cultural customs, adhering to safety precautions, having emergency contacts on hand, and learning about the healthcare facilities that are available. Using the local language and manners will improve your interactions with Riga residents and make for a more enjoyable and memorable trip.

CHAPTER ELEVEN:
Shopping and Souvenirs in Riga

Riga provides a variety of shopping options, including vibrant markets, cutting-edge malls, and one-of-a-kind artisan goods. The following are some highlights for shopping and finding mementos in Riga:

Central Market and Shopping Centers

- Central Market (Centrāltirgus): Situated in the center of Riga, the Central Market is one of the biggest and busiest markets in Europe. It sells a variety of fresh vegetables, regional specialties, apparel, accessories, and household goods out of historic pavilions. Investigate the several markets' sections, each of which is devoted to a certain type of produce, such as fruits, vegetables, meat, fish, dairy goods, and spices. It's a terrific spot to get a taste of the local cuisine, experience traditional Latvian fare, and shop for unusual gifts or kitchen supplies.

- Shopping Centers: Riga is home to a number of cutting-edge shopping malls where you can browse a variety of national and international brands, clothing stores, gadgets, and more. Galerija Centrs, Stockmann, Riga Plaza, and Spice retail Center are some of the most well-known retail centers. These shopping malls provide a convenient and welcoming environment for consumers to shop by housing a range of stores, cafes, restaurants, and entertainment venues.

Artisan Crafts and Souvenir Shops

- Old Town Souvenir Shops: There are several souvenir shops in Riga's Old Town where you may find a large selection of traditional Latvian crafts and mementos. Watch out for stores that sell woven textiles, pottery, hand-knit woolens, amber jewelry, and traditional woodwork crafts. These distinctive and handcrafted goods are ideal presents or mementos of your trip to Riga.

- Bergs Bazaar: This quaint shopping district, which is close to the city center, is well-known for its artisan products and boutique stores. You can find a variety of regional designers, art galleries, antique stores, and specialty businesses here. It's a terrific place to find unique products like handcrafted jewelry, artwork, ceramics, and clothing.

- Latvian Ethnographic Open-Air Museum: Although it is not a typical shopping location, the Latvian Ethnographic Open-Air Museum offers the chance to buy genuine Latvian crafts and traditional products. The museum includes a shop where you may buy handcrafted products including woven baskets, wooden utensils, traditional apparel, and more. It also features ancient houses from several districts of Latvia.

Latvian Amber and Jewelry

In Latvian culture, amber is highly prized and frequently referred to as the country's treasure. Finding amber jewelry and other items created from this ancient resin is very easy in Riga. Amber necklaces, bracelets, earrings, and rings are available in many jewelry stores in Riga. Spend some time perusing the various shops, and think about making a purchase from a trustworthy store that offers certificates of authenticity.

To make an informed purchasing selection when looking for amber or other valuable gemstones, it is advisable to educate yourself on the quality, grading, and cost.

If you make qualified purchases and don't live in the EU, retain your receipts and ask about tax refund alternatives since you may be eligible for a Value Added Tax (VAT) refund after you depart the nation.

Traditional Textiles and Woodwork

- Traditional Textiles: Knitting, intricately woven fabrics, and embroidery are just a few of Latvia's long-standing traditions in the textile industry. You can find exquisitely knitted wool blankets, scarves, mittens, and traditional Latvian costumes in stores that specialize in traditional Latvian textiles. These products display the distinctive designs and themes that are emblematic of Latvian tradition and culture.

- Woodworking: Latvians have a rich history of woodworking, and Riga is a great place to purchase wooden crafts and trinkets. Look for handmade wooden products including carvings, culinary utensils, attractive boxes, and cutting boards. These products showcase the talent and workmanship of Latvian artists and are great for giving or enhancing your home's decor.

Fashion and Design Boutiques

- Miera iela: Peace Street, also known as Miera iela, is renowned for its independent stores and bohemian ambiance. Unique fashion boutiques, design studios, concept businesses, and art galleries fill this trendy boulevard. Discover the wide variety of locally made clothing, accessories, and home products, and encourage upcoming designers from Latvia.

- Kalnciema Quarter: This creative district, which is part of the Agenskalns neighborhood, is home to a variety of artisan workshops, design studios, and boutique stores. It regularly organizes artisan fairs and cultural events, giving visitors the chance to find locally manufactured crafts like ceramics, jewelry, and apparel.

- Riga Fashion Week: Plan your trip to coincide with Riga Fashion Week if you're interested in the fashion scene. Both established and emerging Latvian designers exhibit their designs at this biennial event. It's a wonderful chance to see the ingenuity and talent of the neighborhood fashion scene.

- Shopping Districts: Riga has a variety of shopping areas where you may find both national and international fashion labels. The streets surrounding Riga's Old Town provide a mix of high-street clothes, designer shops, and luxury labels. Elizabetes Street and the neighboring Bergs Bazaar are well renowned for their premium retailers.

Look for one-of-a-kind items that showcase the modern aesthetic and inventiveness of Latvian designers as you browse the fashion and design boutiques in Riga. These shopping areas offer the chance to see the newest styles, help out the local economy, and bring home one-of-a-kind fashion and design goods.

Whether you choose to peruse the vibrant Central Market, look through handcrafted goods and trinkets, or look for distinctive Latvian amber jewelry, shopping in Riga is a joy. Take advantage of the chance to learn about the city's rich cultural legacy and choose the ideal souvenir to keep as a reminder of your trip to Riga.

Whether you choose to explore the world of fashion and design or are looking for traditional textiles and woodwork, Riga provides a bustling shopping environment where you may find unique and memorable things. Spend some time perusing the shops, interacting with the local craftspeople, and taking advantage of the distinctive shopping opportunities Riga has to offer.

CHAPTER TWELVE:
Outdoor Adventures in Riga

In addition to being a city brimming with history and culture, Riga also provides a wide range of outdoor pursuits and adventures. There are many possibilities to embrace nature and enjoy the outdoors, from serene parks and gardens to exhilarating watersports. Here are a few thrilling outdoor activities you may enjoy in Riga:

Parks and Gardens

- Mezaparks: Situated in the city's north, this sizable and gorgeous park has a lake, lovely green areas, and walking paths. It's the perfect location for a leisurely stroll, a picnic with the family, or even a bike trip. The Riga Zoo, which houses a variety of animals from around the world, is also located in Mezaparks.

- Kronvalda Park is a tranquil urban paradise with well-kept lawns, flowerbeds, and tree-lined walks that is close to the Riga Old Town. The park is a well-liked location for leisurely strolls, outdoor fitness, and taking in views of the close-by canal. You can rent paddleboats in the summer or have a picnic on the grassy areas.

- Vermanes Garden: A quaint, tranquil public park in the heart of the city, Vermanes Garden is a great place to relax. It features plenty of lush vegetation, vibrant flowerbeds, and chairs where you may relax. Throughout the summer, the park also hosts a number of cultural gatherings and live concerts.

Riga Canal and Daugava River

- Riga Canal: The Riga Canal, which runs through the center of the city, provides picturesque views and a serene ambiance. You can stroll leisurely along the canal's edges, hire a rowboat or pedal boat, or just sit back and unwind on a seat and observe the passing boats. When the nearby trees and flowers are in full bloom in the spring and summer, the canal is especially attractive.

- Daugava River: The Daugava River is a significant waterway that passes through Riga and offers a variety of chances for water sports. You can hire a kayak or paddleboard and explore the river at your own speed, or you can take a river cruise to take in panoramic views of the city skyline. Some businesses also provide boat cruises to adjacent islands during the summer, giving you the chance to take in the river's and its surrounds' natural beauty.

Cycling and Segway Tours

A fun and environmentally friendly way to visit Riga is by bicycle. Renting a bicycle will allow you to explore the city's icons and secret attractions at your own leisure as you peddle along the designated bike lanes. As an alternative, think about taking a Segway tour if you're searching for an interesting and convenient way to explore. With the help of an experienced guide, you can easily navigate the city while learning about its history and culture.

Watersports and Sailing

Riga provides a variety of watersports activities for the daring. Along the Baltic Sea coast, you can practice windsurfing, kiteboarding, or stand-up paddling. All skill levels can participate thanks to the availability of introductory lessons and equipment rentals. Consider going sailing on the Baltic Sea and taking in the stunning vistas of the shoreline if you're seeking for a more tranquil experience.

Winter Activities and Ice Skating

Riga transforms into a winter paradise in the winter and offers a wide range of outdoor recreation opportunities. There are many outdoor ice skating rinks in the city where you may skate on the ice while admiring the picturesque winter landscape. The rink in Esplanade Park and the Lido Recreation Center are two of the most well-liked places to go ice skating. Additionally, you may do cross-country skiing in the city's parks or go downhill skiing and snowboarding at surrounding ski resorts.

The outdoor activities in Riga are suitable for a range of interests and seasons, enabling tourists to take in the scenery and partake in exhilarating pursuits. Riga offers a variety of opportunities to enjoy the great outdoors, whether you like quiet strolls through parks, exploring the city's waterways, cycling through the streets, or participating in winter sports.

CHAPTER THIRTEEN:
Riga's Annual Events and Festivals:

Riga is a city that enjoys partying, and it hosts a wide variety of events and festivals throughout the year to highlight its rich cultural heritage, customs, and vivacious attitude. Here are three festivals and events that take place every year in Riga and draw both residents and tourists:

Riga City Festival

The Riga City Festival is a yearly event that takes place in August and turns the city into a vibrant center of art, music, dancing, and entertainment. This three-day festival offers a variety of events for people of all ages while showcasing the best of Riga's cultural scene. Open-air concerts, local artists' performances, dance performances, art exhibits, food vendors, and numerous sporting events are all part of the festival. Visitors can stroll around Riga's busy streets, take in the festive ambiance, and sense the city's vivid vitality.

Latvian Song and Dance Festival

Every five years, Riga hosts the Latvian Song and Dance Festival, a prominent cultural occasion. Thousands of singers, dancers, musicians, and audience members from Latvia and other countries participate in it. This lavish display of Latvian folk song and dance is a source of great national pride and is deeply ingrained in the nation's cultural history. Impressive choir performances, folk dance demonstrations, concerts of traditional music, and other cultural events are all part of the festival. It's a rare chance to see the harmony and beauty of Latvian cultural traditions.

Riga Christmas Market

Every year, in the center of Riga's Old Town, during the holiday season, the Riga Christmas Market is a cherished tradition. It turns the city into a mystical winter paradise and charms tourists with its jovial attitude. The market has a large number of booths selling handcrafted goods, vintage Christmas decorations, regional specialties, and chilly beverages like mulled wine and gingerbread. Visitors can stroll through the market, try regional cuisine, look for one-of-a-kind presents, and take in live folk and Christmas music performances. A beautiful event that perfectly captures the spirit of the festive season is the Riga Christmas Market.

Summer Solstice Celebrations

Jāņi, or the Summer Solstice, is a customary Latvian event honoring the beginning of summer. Around

June 23, the longest day of the year, Riga celebrates this joyous event with vivacious festivities. You can participate in the ages-old, passed-down paganism-inspired rituals and practices associated with the Summer Solstice celebrations. Building bonfires, singing folk songs, and partaking in other folk games and rituals are common activities that people engage in when they congregate in parks, gardens, and rural places. People wear flower crowns and consume traditional foods including cheese, caraway seed buns, and beer. The celebrations of the Summer Solstice in Riga provide a singular window into Latvian culture and its close ties to the natural world.

International Music Festivals

Riga is home to a number of renowned music festivals that draw visitors from all over the world, including musicians and festival goers. These events feature a wide variety of musical styles, such as jazz, contemporary, and alternative. The following Riga-based music festivals are noteworthy:

- Riga Jurmala Music Festival: The famed Riga Jurmala Music Festival, which takes place in the summer and comprises top-notch orchestras, conductors, and singers. The festival offers a variety of musical performances at revered locations like Jurmala, a nearby resort town, and its Great Guild Hall and Dzintari Concert Hall. Exceptional performances of symphonies, chamber music, and operas by renowned musicians and ensembles are available to audiences.

- Positivus Festival: As the largest music and arts event in the Baltics, Positivus Festival draws a wide range of musicians from around the world and the region. The festival, which is just outside of Riga in the charming coastal town of Salacgrīva, has a diverse range of musical styles, including rock, pop, indie, techno, and more. Positivus includes music concerts, workshops, and art installations in addition to a laid-back camping setting.

- Riga Jazz Festival: Jazz fans will find their groove at the Riga Jazz Festival, which features both seasoned and up-and-coming jazz musicians. Several locations in Riga, including the Riga Congress Hall and the Latvian Radio Studio 1, host the festival. Concerts cover a broad variety of jazz styles and improvisation in settings ranging from small jazz club settings to large-scale productions.

These yearly celebrations and events in Riga bring the city's cultural diversity to light and foster harmony and joy among its citizens and guests. Riga's Summer Solstice celebrations and international music offer memorable experiences that highlight the vibrant spirit of the city's cultural scene, whether you attend the Riga City Festival to immerse yourself in the city's artistic expressions, take in the grandeur of the Latvian Song and Dance Festival, or stroll through the charming Riga Christmas Market.

CHAPTER FOURTEEN:
Riga for Art and History Lovers

The city of Riga is rich in both art and history and has a wide variety of sights and experiences to offer both art and history fans. Riga offers visitors a diverse cultural tapestry to discover and enjoy, ranging from historical museums and key World War II locations to art galleries and exhibitions.

Art Galleries and Exhibitions

With various galleries and shows displaying a wide variety of artistic styles and mediums, Riga is home to a thriving art scene. Several renowned art galleries are:

- Riga Art Space: Located in the center of the city, Riga Art Space is a venue for contemporary art that regularly holds exhibitions by both domestic and foreign artists. Modern art, such as paintings, sculptures, photographs, and multimedia works, is the gallery's main focus.

- Latvian National Museum of Art: The Latvian National Museum of Art is home to a sizable collection of Latvian artwork from the medieval era to the present. The museum displays pieces by well-known Latvian painters and additionally conducts transient exhibitions that investigate various artistic themes and movements.

- Arsenal Museum of modern Art: This museum displays modern artwork from across the world and from Latvia in the historic Arsenal building. It contains a sizable collection of contemporary works of art, including paintings, sculptures, installations, and video art.

These galleries provide visitors a look at Riga's thriving art scene and give both well-known and up-and-coming artists a place to showcase their works.

Riga History Museums

Riga is a city with a rich history that dates back centuries. History enthusiasts can delve into the city's past through its numerous history museums, where artifacts, exhibitions, and interactive displays bring history to life. Some notable history museums in Riga include:

- The Latvian National Museum of History offers a thorough overview of Latvian history from the prehistoric era to the present. It has a broad variety of historical relics, including discoveries from archaeology, ethnographic items, and records that tell the history of the nation.

- Museum of the Occupation of Latvia: This museum explores Latvia's 20th-century occupation by the Soviet Union and Nazi Germany. Through a selection of images, records, and firsthand accounts, it provides a thorough picture of the political, social, and cultural impacts of these times on Latvian society.

- Riga Motor Museum: The Riga Motor Museum is largely devoted to the history of automobiles, but it also provides insights into the larger historical setting of the 20th century. It displays a variety of antique automobiles, motorbikes, and other vehicles, illustrating the social and technological advances that took place at the time.

World War II History Sites

Several historically significant locations in Riga represent this chaotic era and have a crucial relation to World War II. These websites provide information on how the war affected the city and its residents. Famous World War II historical locations in Riga include:

- Riga Ghetto and Latvian Holocaust Museum: The old Jewish ghetto region now houses the Riga Ghetto and Latvian Holocaust Museum, which offers a grim look back at the Holocaust in Latvia. It draws attention to the plight of the Jewish community and informs visitors of the war's atrocities.

- Freedom Monument: Although it is unrelated to World War II particularly, the Freedom Monument serves as a representation of Latvia's ongoing struggle for freedom. As a memorial for the sacrifices made during the war and the later occupation times, it is of utmost importance.

- Riga Aviation Museum: This museum presents Latvian aviation history, particularly the nation's participation in World War II. It exhibits wartime aircraft and offers details on Latvia's contribution to aviation technology and military activities.

Soviet Heritage and Architecture

Riga still carries remnants of its Soviet past, and learning more about the city's history is fascinating for history buffs. Riga underwent enormous urban and architectural development throughout the Soviet era, and is now known for its imposing buildings and big monuments. In Riga, noteworthy Soviet-era landmarks and architectural sites include:

- Academy of Sciences Building: The Academy of Sciences Building, also referred to as "Stalin's Birthday Cake," is a notable example of Soviet-era architecture. Its characteristic Stalinist architecture includes elaborate embellishments and a panoramic viewing platform with stunning city views.

- Victory Monument: This imposing building was erected to honor Latvia's triumph over Nazi Germany during World War II, and it is a significant reminder of Soviet-era remembrance. A statue of a lady holding three stars—the three Baltic states—stands in for the monument.

- Spikeri Quarter: Originally a warehouse zone, the Spikeri Quarter has evolved into a thriving center for culture and the arts. It features modern art galleries, retail stores, and cultural institutions with industrial buildings from the Soviet era.

It is possible to learn more about Riga's complicated history and the city's transition from Soviet domination to independence by visiting these architectural icons and buildings with Soviet heritage.

Riga's Art Nouveau Heritage

The magnificent Art Nouveau architecture in Riga, which flourished in the early 20th century, is well known. With more than 800 buildings featuring elaborate facades, ornate accents, and distinctive aesthetic expressions, the city is home to one of the biggest collections of Art Nouveau buildings in the world. The following are notable examples of Riga's Art Nouveau legacy:

- Alberta iela: The Art Nouveau district of Riga is thought to be concentrated here. While strolling around Alberta iela, you'll come across a variety of magnificent structures embellished with rich sculptures, exquisite embellishments, and unique designs.

- Riga Art Nouveau Museum: The Riga Art Nouveau Museum, housed in a stunningly maintained Art Nouveau structure, provides a thorough overview of the Art Nouveau movement in Riga. Visitors can tour the museum's period-appropriate interior and discover more about the artisans and architects that helped to preserve the city's Art Nouveau tradition.

- Elizabetes iela: Elizabetes iela is a street adorned with excellent specimens of Art Nouveau architecture and is another street famed for its Art Nouveau structures. The facades include stunning symmetry, fantastical creatures, and elaborate floral motifs.

The Art Nouveau architecture in Riga is evidence of the city's artistic and architectural supremacy in the early 20th century. Art and history enthusiasts can appreciate the beauty and craftsmanship of this renowned architectural movement by exploring these amazing structures.

Finally, Riga provides a fascinating fusion of art and history for explorers to discover. The city offers a plethora of cultural and historical assets that give a vivid picture of its past and present, from its art galleries and exhibitions to its history museums, World War II locations, Soviet heritage, and Art Nouveau architecture. Riga offers a genuinely immersive experience for art and history lovers, whether you're charmed by modern art, interested by the city's stormy history, or mesmerized by architectural wonders.

CHAPTER FIFTEEN:
Conclusion and Farewell to Riga

The time has come to take stock of the fascinating encounters, rich cultural heritage, and priceless experiences you have had while traveling through Riga. Riga has definitely made an everlasting impression on your vacation memories with its unique blend of history, art, delectable cuisine, and kind hospitality.

You have learned about the mesmerizing charm of Riga's Old Town, strolled through the lively Central Market, and immersed yourself in the alluring Art Nouveau neighborhood during your journey of Riga. You have appreciated the splendor of Riga Castle, St. Peter's Church, and Riga Cathedral's architecture, as well as exploring off the beaten path to find undiscovered gems like Riga Art Space and Kalnciema Quarter.

You have been completely immersed in Riga's rich cultural heritage, whether it be through the spectacular operatic productions at the Latvian National Opera, the fascinating exhibits at the city's art and history museums, or the colorful folklore and customs that have been passed down through the years. You have indulged in street food treats from the neighborhood markets, tasted the tastes of Latvian cuisine, and watched energetic traditional dance and music performances that mesmerize you with their rhythm and enthusiasm.

The natural splendor of Sigulda and Gauja National Parks, the medieval attraction of Cesis Castle, and the tranquil seaside attractiveness of Jurmala Beach were among the fascinating day trips you took outside the city limits. You have taken advantage of Riga's outdoor activities, whether it be by strolls through its parks and gardens, peaceful boat rides along the Daugava River and Riga Canal, or exhilarating cycling and segway trips.

You've been mesmerized by the spirit of Riga's yearly celebrations and events, including the exuberant Riga City Festival, the breathtaking Latvian Song and Dance Festival, the enchanted Riga Christmas Market, the jubilant Summer Solstice Celebrations, and the highly regarded music festivals that have enlivened the city with melody and joy.

You take with you the memories of Riga's cultural gems, the friendliness of its residents, and the allure of its streets as you say goodbye to the city. Your awareness of this amazing city and its position in the world will be forever enriched by the experiences and information you obtained while you were in Riga.

May the spirit of Riga's history, art, culture, and hospitality continue to inspire you whether you visit the city again in the future or go on new experiences abroad. Say goodbye to Riga, a place that embraced you with wide arms and left a lasting impression on your heart and spirit. May your travels be full of wonder, discovery, and life-changing events till we meet again.

Safe travels and fond memories, dear traveler.

CHAPTER SIXTEEN: Appendix

In this appendix, you will find useful information to enhance your experience in Riga. Here are updated details on 30 Latvian language phrases and pronunciations, a currency conversion chart, and a packing list tailored specifically for your trip to Riga.

30 Latvian Language Phrases with Pronunciations Guide

While many Latvians speak English, learning a few basic Latvian phrases can greatly enrich your interactions and show your appreciation for the local culture. Here are some commonly used phrases along with their pronunciations:

1. Hello - Sveiki (SVEY-kee)

2. Goodbye - Uz redzēšanos (ooz rehd-ZEH-shah-nohs)

3. Thank you - Paldies (PUHL-dee-es)

4. Please - Lūdzu (LOO-dzoo)

5. Excuse me - Atvainojiet (aht-vah-EE-noh-yet)

6. Yes - Jā (yaa)

7. No - Nē (ney)

8. Sorry - Atvainojiet (aht-vah-EE-noh-yet)

9. I don't understand - Es nesaprotu (es neh-sah-PROH-too)

10. Could you help me? - Vai jūs varētu man palīdzēt? (vai yoos vah-REH-too mahn pah-LEE-dzeyt)

11. Where is...? - Kur ir...? (koor eer)

12. How much does it cost? - Cik tas maksā? (tsihk tahs mahk-sah)

13. Do you speak English? - Vai jūs runājat angļu valodā? (vai yoos roo-NAH-yat ahng-loo VAH-loh-dah)

14. I would like... - Es vēlētos... (es VEH-leh-tohs)

15. Can I have the menu? - Vai es varu saņemt ēdienkarti? (vai es vah-roo sah-nyehmt EH-dee-yehn-kahr-tee)

16. Cheers! - Priekā! (pree-EH-kah)

17. Where is the restroom? - Kur ir tualete? (koor eer too-ah-LEH-teh)

18. I love Riga - Es mīlu Rīgu (es MEE-loo REE-goo)

19. What time is it? - Cik ir pulkstenis? (tsihk eer PUHL-kstenis)

20. Can you recommend a good restaurant? - Vai jūs varat ieteikt labu restorānu? (vai yoos VAH-raht yeh-teykt LAH-boo rehs-toh-RAH-noo)

21. Where can I find a taxi? - Kur es varu atrast taksometru? (koor es vah-roo ah-trahst tahk-soh-MEH-troo)

22. I'm lost - Es esmu pazudis (es EHS-moo pah-ZOO-dees)

23. How do I get to...? - Kā nokļūt uz...? (kah noh-KLOOT oos)

24. What is your name? - Kā jūs sauc? (kah yoos sauts)

25. My name is... - Mani sauc... (mah-nee sauts)

26. I'm sorry, I don't speak Latvian well - Atvainojiet, es nezinu latviešu valodu labi (aht-vah-EE-noh-yet, es neh-ZEE-noo LAHT-vyeh-shoo VAH-loh-doo LAH-bee)

27. Can you take a photo of me, please? - Vai jūs varat mani fotografēt, lūdzu? (vai yoos VAH-raht mah-nee foh-toh-grah-FEHT, LOO-dzoo)

28. What is this? - Kas tas ir? (kahs tahs eer)

29. Help! - Palīdzība! (pah-LEE-dzee-bah)

30. Have a nice day! - Jauku dienu! (YAH-oo-koo dee-eh-noo)

This is just a selection of phrases. Feel free to learn more Latvian phrases to enhance your communication during your time in Riga. Remember, learning a few basic phrases is a great way to show respect for the local culture and connect with the people you meet during your time in Riga.

Note: Pronunciations provided above are approximate and may vary based on individual accents and dialects. It is recommended to listen to audio recordings or seek assistance from locals for precise pronunciation.

Currency Conversion Chart

Knowing the currency exchange rates can help you manage your finances effectively. Here is an updated currency conversion chart to convert Latvian Lat (LVL) to your local currency or any other preferred currency:

- 1 EUR = 0.7028 LVL
- 1 USD = 0.6143 LVL
- 1 GBP = 0.8422 LVL

- 1 AUD = 0.4441 LVL
- 1 CAD = 0.4978 LVL

Please note that currency exchange rates may vary, so it's recommended to check for updated rates before making any financial transactions.

Packing List for Riga

To ensure you are well-prepared for your trip to Riga, here is a comprehensive packing list:

Clothing:
  - Comfortable walking shoes
  - Light jacket or sweater (even in summer, evenings can be cooler)
  - Raincoat or umbrella (as Riga can experience rain throughout the year)
  - Swimwear and beach towel (if visiting in the summer)

Essentials:
- Valid passport and necessary travel documents
- Travel adapter and chargers for electronic devices
- Local currency or credit/debit cards
- Travel insurance documents
- Portable power bank for charging devices on the go

Personal Items:
- Medications (if required)
- Toiletries (including sunscreen, insect repellent, and any specific personal care items)
- Basic first aid kit

Electronics:
- Camera or smartphone for capturing memories
- Portable device for accessing maps and travel information
- E-reader or books for leisure reading

Miscellaneous:

- Travel guidebook or map of Riga
- Reusable water bottle
- Snacks for on-the-go
- Day bag or backpack for daily excursions

Remember to pack according to the season and activities you plan to engage in during your stay in Riga.

By utilizing these helpful resources, including the Latvian language phrases, currency conversion chart, and packing list, you'll be well-prepared to make the most of your time in Riga. Enjoy your trip and immerse yourself in the beauty and charm of this remarkable city.

MAP OF RIGA

Printed by Amazon Italia Logistica S.r.l.
Torrazza Piemonte (TO), Italy

60945985R00087